THE HUMAN ERROR PLAYS

1

THE HUMAN ERROR PLAYS
by J. A. Gucci

TABLE OF CONTENTS

The Paradox Poundcake

7

CHARACTERS

MAN — A polite, logical, increasingly confused customer.
BAKER — Calm, precise, unwaveringly confident.

SETTING

A boutique bakery, late morning. Cozy shelves. Chalkboard menu. A bell jingles as the MAN enters. A single poundcake rests under a glass dome.

BAKER
Good morning, sir!
Welcome to The Villa—

MAN
I come here all the time,
you must be new.

BAKER
New owner, yes.
Since I bought the place—
eight…no, ten…

MAN
Eleven?
(pause)
How much for the cookies?

BAKER
Twelve!

MAN
Twelve is steep.

BAKER
Twelve days ago.
(beat)
What can I get you today?
Cookies?

MAN
Nice try.
I think I'll have—

(he drifts, lost in thought)

BAKER
Croissant?
Cheese Danish?

MAN
Tira—mi—

BAKER
Poundcake?

MAN
—su.

(snaps out of it)

BAKER
Plain or blueberry mascarpone.

MAN
Blueberry mascarpone.
What'll that cost me?

BAKER
One dollar per pound.

MAN
And if I want…
two percent filling?

BAKER
Twenty-four dollars a pound.

MAN
That's absurd.

BAKER
Here you go—
one pound of cake
with blueberry mascarpone filling.

MAN
Are you sure it's a pound?

BAKER
Weighed it myself.
One pound,
one percent filling.

MAN
Weigh it again.

(He does)

BAKER
Still one pound.

MAN
Alright.
Make it two percent.

BAKER
With pleasure.

(He produces a visibly smaller cake.)

Here you are—
one pound of cake,
two percent filling.

MAN
Wait—
this is half the size of the first!

BAKER
That's right.
One pound of cake—
two percent filling.
Ninety-eight percent cake.

MAN
That makes no sense.

BAKER
It's mathematics.

MAN
I want my money back.

BAKER
No refunds.

MAN
Half back then.

BAKER
No exchanges.

*(long silence. The MAN stares at the shrinking cake.
From beneath the counter, a low buttery voice rises.)*

POUNDCAKE
Next time…
just take the box.

(Blackout.)

The Accountant Paradox

*"The accountant files returns for all and only those who
do not file their own. So—who files his?"*

CHARACTERS

FRED – A bureaucratic accountant, paradoxical by nature.
TIM – An anxious taxpayer seeking a refund to survive.

SETTING

An unremarkable accountant's office. A desk.
A stack of folders. A pen that squeaks.

FRED
Zero. Zip. Zilch.

TIM
You're a lousy accountant, Fred.

FRED
It's not me, Tim—
your earnings are too high.

TIM
I was counting on that refund
to pay the mortgage.

FRED
No available entries.

TIM
Smear a number or two.

FRED
Sorry—
I'm a straight shooter, Tim.

TIM
I'll lose my house, Fred.

FRED
Do your own taxes then.
I only file returns
for people who do not file their own.

TIM
Is that hard to do?

FRED
Yes—
and that's why
I always file my own taxes…
through someone else.

TIM
Wait—who does your taxes, Fred?

FRED
Not me. That's for sure.

TIM
What about the guy down the street—
Lawrence, I think his name is?

FRED
I don't know.

TIM
I'll go see Lawrence.
I bet he can do a better job than you.

FRED
That's the DIY spirit, Tim!

TIM
How hard can it be?
Just fill in the blanks, right?

FRED
That's right—
fill them in
however you like.
And when Lawrence misfiles—
it's the slammer, pal.

(Pause)

TIM (to audience)
Lawrence isn't afraid to
smudge a number here and there.
Everyone does it, I am sure.
He understands—
honest people
honestly earning
an honest buck
smudge—
with scruples.
Survival is only natural.
Lawrence understands—
the human condition.

(Beat. TIM stares at the page, then looks past it.)

I wonder—
who will prevail—
the little guy
protecting his
little house—
or
the bureaucratic Big House—
protecting
its
big ideals.

(He holds the form gently, almost reverently.)

Smudge a number
smear a record—
pray
for me,
Frank.

FRED
Let me know if you run into trouble—
filing's tricky.

TIM *(to Frank)*
How long does it take
to file your own taxes?

FRED
Depends who you ask.
If you ask Lawrence?
About 11 hours and 47 minutes—

though technically,
I don't do them.
My accountant handles it.

TIM
You mean Frank?

FRED
Tim—
whoever that is…

TIM
Settled, then.

FRED
Don't forget to sign a name.

TIM
Whose name?

FRED
Not yours.

(Blackout.)

Sold

19

CHARACTERS

MAN – Nervous, rational, but gradually unravels.
MECHANIC – Calm, persuasive, ominously
bureaucratic

SETTING

A garage. A car is on a lift. Papers, coffee, and a
faint hum of machines. The air smells of rubber and
fate.

MECHANIC
It's your car,
your money,
your decision.
(*pause*)
Replace?
Or repair?

(*silence*)

MAN
If I choose to repair—

MECHANIC
It'll cost you half as much.

MAN
If choose to replace—

MECHANIC
It'll cost you half—
as much.

(silence)

MAN
Okay.
Replace it is, then.
(beat)
I'm having a blood transfusion
day after tomorrow—

MECHANIC
And you can't keep that on ice
too long, right?

MAN
Exactly.

MECHANIC
It'll run like new.
More than that—
it'll be a whole new car.
(beat)
Just like you.
New blood,
new man.
(pause)
Now—
sign here.
Come back tomorrow—
I'll let you take it for a test drive.

MAN
What exactly are you replacing?
And how are you going to do it?

(silence)

MECHANIC
Well…
The Observed Protocol for the Remediation
of a Circumferential Vehicular Pressure Failure
Event is as follows—

MAN
Okay, okay—
I get it.
(beat)
You're going to replace the broken part.

MECHANIC
You've got a flat, pal.
I'll put on a new tire.

(Next day. The MAN returns. The air feels different. Too clean.)

MECHANIC
What are you doing here?

MAN
I came to pick up my "new" car.

MECHANIC
Would you like to test drive it?

MAN
I'm sure it's fine.
How much do I owe you?

MECHANIC
$175,000 please.

MAN
What!?
To replace a tire?

MECHANIC
Replace—erase.
One bolt turned—
a world reborn.
(pause)
We take cash only.

(silence)

MAN
I'm a dead man.

MECHANIC
Sold.

(Blackout.)

The Impossible Lie

CHARACTERS

PROSECUTOR – Stern, increasingly exasperated.
MR. FALSEHOOD – Slippery, smug, evasive.
MR. WRIGHT – Quiet, confused, unpredictably poetic.
THE HAT – A silent witness. Speaks only once.

SETTING

A surreal courtroom. One spotlight on a worn wooden chair.
MR. FALSEHOOD sits center.
MR. WRIGHT stands by the witness box, wearing a corduroy hat.
The Hat sits squarely atop his head.

PROSECUTOR
Mr. Falsehood—
are you trustworthy?

MR. FALSEHOOD
Yes.
I always tell the truth.

PROSECUTOR
Did you steal the chocolate?

MR. FALSEHOOD
What kind is it?

PROSECUTOR
Why does that matter?

MR. FALSEHOOD
If it's got peanuts—
it wasn't me.

PROSECUTOR
A witness says they saw you.

MR. FALSEHOOD
Did you check his vision?

PROSECUTOR (*to Mr. Wright*)
How many fingers am I holding up?

MR. FALSEHOOD
See?
He's blind.

PROSECUTOR
Mr. Wright?

MR. FALSEHOOD
And deaf.

MR. WRIGHT
I'm sorry—
did somebody say something?

MR. FALSEHOOD
Get off the stand, pal.

PROSECUTOR
You're the one on trial.
And it's Death Row.
This is no laughing matter.

MR. FALSEHOOD
And that hat—
no one can see straight
in corduroy.

MR. WRIGHT
I'm not declaring
to be the captain of Illinois.

PROSECUTOR
Mr. Wright—
does your hat obstruct your sight?

MR. WRIGHT
Well…
I've never been on a spaceflight,
so… I don't know.

MR. FALSEHOOD
See?
Ask the hat.
Maybe that'll clear things up.

PROSECUTOR
I'll handle this,
Mr. Falsehood.

(reaches for the hat)

PROSECUTOR
(to Mr. Wright)
Do you mind?

MR. WRIGHT
No, sir.
I am not blind.

PROSECUTOR (to the hat)
Did you
see
Mr. Falsehood
steal
the chocolate?

(Silence. All eyes on the hat.)

PROSECUTOR
Well?

MR. FALSEHOOD
Alright, look—
no offense, Pops—
I did it.
Happy now?

PROSECUTOR
You're admitting
to stealing the chocolate.

MR. FALSEHOOD
No.
That was a lie.

PROSECUTOR
This is perjury!

MR. FALSEHOOD
I'm telling the truth.

THE HAT
Peanuts.

(Black out.)

Just Be Yourself
A Short Absurdist Dialogue

CHARACTERS

HOST — Cheerful, oblivious, repeats the refrain "Just be yourselves."
MAN 1 — Polite, then overperforms as a doctor, unraveling into maternal resentment.
MAN 2 — Polite, then overperforms as an attorney, unraveling into fractured identity.
WOMAN — Polite, then overperforms as the perfect caretaker, unraveling into domestic inadequacy.
GUN — A confetti party gun with agency. Flat, ominous, disruptive.

SETTING

A cocktail party. A pleasant living room with hors d'oeuvres on trays, string lights, a disco ball, and ambient jazz. Guests mill about in the background.

(A confetti party gun fires in the air with a celebratory POP. Glitter rains down. Guests laugh lightly in the background.)

HOST
Welcome, everyone!
Please—enjoy the party.
No need to be shy.
Just be yourselves.

MAN 1
Hello.

WOMAN
Hi there.

MAN 2
Good evening.

(A brief, polite pause.)

WOMAN
Lovely gathering.

MAN 2
Very nice.

MAN 1
Yes, indeed.

(Another pause. Slight tension.)

WOMAN
Whoopsies!

MAN 1
(perking up suddenly)
Perhaps I should take your temperature.
I happen to be a rather brilliant neurosurgeon.

MAN 2
I noticed your walking cane—
Did you fall

WOMAN
Looks like someone spilled their wine!

MAN 1
You look pale, ma'am.
This will only take a second.

MAN 2
Where exactly did you fall?

WOMAN
Here, let me tidy that jacket.

MAN 1
There we are—
Open wide…

MAN 2
I can assist you.
I'm an injury attorney, actually.

WOMAN
All squeaky clean now!

MAN 1
Let's try again, shall we?

MAN 2
Was the fall an accident, or…?

WOMAN
Let's tuck this little napkin under your chin—
just in case.

MAN 1
Open up…

MAN 2
Suit yourself—
You might've had a case,
but you just blew it.

WOMAN
Neat and tidy!

HOST
(cheerfully interrupting)
Everyone—please!
No need to be shy.
Just be yourselves!

GUN
(cutting in, flat)
Who wants to play—
roulette?

(A beat. The lighting begins to dim. Jazz slows.
Guests in the background fade into stillness. The
tone shifts from surface cheer to deeper unraveling.)

————

UNRAVELING

MAN 2
Mauled—
by a Maltese.

WOMAN
No good.

MAN 1
I never wanted to be a doctor.

MAN 2
Torn apart:
flesh
from limb.

WOMAN
At friendship.

MAN 1
I only did it to appease my mother.

MAN 2
Debonair to distortion.

WOMAN
At making money.

MAN 1
I loathe her.

MAN 2
A body—
replaced—

WOMAN
At housekeeping.

MAN 1
I'm waiting for her to die.

MAN 2
By grafting.

WOMAN
At mothering.

MAN 1
So I could live.

MAN 2
Masks—

WOMAN
At love.

MAN 1
I can't take it anymore.

MAN 2
Layered over masks.

WOMAN
At cooking.

MAN 1
I'll take her life.

MAN 2
Identity.

WOMAN
No good.

MAN 1
I'll take my life.

MAN 2
Dissolution.

WOMAN
Inadequate.

MAN 1
I'm so confused.

MAN 2
I no longer remember—

WOMAN
Could you take my life—
after you're done taking yours?

MAN 1
What to do...

MAN 2
I.

WOMAN
(*softly, almost childlike*)
Pretty please?

HOST
(*brightly, as if none of that happened*)
Everyone—please!
No need to be shy.
Just be yourselves!

GUN
(*cocks, ominous*)
Any takers?

———

REWIND

(*Suddenly, everything rewinds in fast motion: lights brighten, jazz resumes, guests murmur again. The trio reset, stiff and polite. They begin again, exactly as before.*)

MAN 1
Hello.

WOMAN
Hi there.

MAN 2
Good evening.

(*A brief pause.*)

WOMAN
Lovely gathering.

MAN 2
Very nice.

MAN 1
Yes, indeed.

HOST
(*cheerful, bright — cutting through*)
Everyone—please!
No need to be shy.
Just be yourselves!

GUN
(*flat, final*)
Never mind.
Time already pulled the trigger.

(Silence. Lights snap out.)

(Blackout.)

The Thermostat
or, The Calibration of Certainty

43

CHARACTERS

A — Lightly dressed, confident in facts, committed to interpretation over sensation.
B — Heavily bundled, experiential, intuitive, increasingly metaphysical.
THE THERMOSTAT — Illegible. Inert. Absolute authority. (Never speaks.)

SETTING

A run-down apartment. It might be too hot, or too cold; only the illegible thermostat knows.
A radiator hums faintly, or not at all.
A wears shorts, a tank top, and flip-flops.
B is bundled in layers.
The lighting is flat, uncertain—halfway between day and night.)

A
(*gazing at radiator*)
Hm.

B
No.
(*shivers*)
Brr.

A
No need for dramatics.

B
Drama?
(beat)
This room is a Bootes Void.

A
I'll have it fixed in no time.

B
Then you're already late.

A
The clock is frozen, remember?

B
My memory is frozen, remember?

(pause)

A
Did you check the thermostat?

(They cross to an old, blurred thermostat on the wall.)

B
(confidently, pointing)
Yes. It says—sixteen degrees.

(pause)

A
(squinting)
That's not a one,
nor is that a six.

B
What is it then?

A
It says—
(beat)
seventy-nine degrees.

B
How could you tell?

A
Facts are facts.

B
The numbers are smeared, though.

A
Then it's probably sixteen degrees.

B
Yes! The data speaks for itself.

A
How could you be so sure?

B
Facts are facts are facts.

A
But the numbers are smudged.

B
The radiator isn't making any noise.
Radiators are supposed to keep you up at night—
so it must be sixteen degrees.

A
Aha!

B
Aha what?

A
(checks the watch that isn't there)
It's the afternoon.

B
(pointing out the fogged window)
No— the sun has already set.

A
(looking out the same window)
Looks like afternoon to me.

B
Where is the sun, then?

A
Behind that skinny building
next to the smaller, rounder one.

B
The skinny thing is a one—
the smaller round thing is a six.
Sixteen—made of window frost
and a coiled vine.
(silence)

A
Let's wait until night,
when the radiator starts making noise.
Then we'll know what the temperature is.

B
Okay. Fine.

(They sit in two chairs, staring at each other. Long silence.)

A
Do you have time?

(pause)

B
Yes.

(silence)

A
Well?

B
Well what?

A
The time.

B
What about it?

A
Aren't you going to give it to me?

B
I don't have the time.

(silence)

A
Why not?

B
It's frozen.

A
Where?
(beat)

B
Bootes Void.

*(Lights fade to blue-black. The faint hum stops.
Silence.)*

(Blackout.)

The Red Blotch
An Absurdist Monologue

CHARACTERS

THE SPEAKER — Any gender. Intelligent, articulate, and deeply paranoid. A rational mind spiraling through self-diagnosis, ritual, and catastrophic logic.
THE BLOTCH — A one-millimeter anomaly. Silent. Expanding. Possibly imagined. (Never speaks.)

SETTING

A cluttered, paranoid household—lab gear, hazmat suit, maybe a red spiral drawn on the wall. The tone is manic, suspicious, and theatrical.

(The Speaker steps forward, clutching their wrist, eyes wild with theory.)

SPEAKER
I wonder from which parallel universe
this little red blotch on my wrist came—
it wasn't there yesterday,
or the day before—
it's growing wild like an afro.

I measured it:
precisely one millimeter long,
one millimeter wide,
and one millimeter high.

I even sketched it—
in red ink—
to match its weird little Fibonacci spiral,
in case something happens.

(Leans forward, whispering like it's a secret.)
An accidental burn that smears it…
or worse:
an amputation
via butcher knife and sneeze.

(Back upright, proud.)
Just in case the doctor misplaces my test results
and can no longer identify the anomaly.

(Pulls out a makeshift prop or gestures grandly.)
I now keep my wrist in an incubator—
the same one I used last week
for my diseased foot
that wouldn't stop itching.

Probably internal hemorrhaging
my podiatrist missed.
My neurologist says it's athlete's foot.
But I won't accept that BS—
I'm not an athlete.

And what does a neurologist
know about feet
anyway?

I am currently awaiting the veterinarian.
She refused at first—
apparently,
I am "not an animal."

(Shrugs—knowingly.)

I explained, calmly,
that we are all animals:
grotesque, decaying, hairy bags of water.

She hung up on me.
Still—
I'm confident she'll arrive shortly.

(Gestures to their hazmat suit.)
The hazmat suit I'm wearing?
It's to prevent the 1x1x1 mystery blotch
from contaminating the environment—
causing an outbreak,
an epidemic,
or worse:

a wide-spread,
irreversible
plague.

(Beat. Then suddenly still.)
The house is surely infected.
I've prepared a contingency plan
involving gasoline and a spark.
I will burn it all down
and watch from the outhouse.

(Smiles.)
Mission accomplished.
(Softly. A new curiosity awakening…)
At last,
I can remove this unbearably hot hazmat suit—
and begin the examination anew:

(Back to the beginning, as if in a loop.)
I wonder from which parallel universe
this little red blotch on my wrist came…

(Blackout.)

Live Animal
An Absurdist Micro-Play

57

CHARACTERS

GIRL — Curious, intuitive, emotionally porous.
Moves easily between play, fear, and poetic
abstraction.
BOY — Analytical, performative, conspiratorial.
Uses logic, props, and bravado to mask uncertainty.
THE BOX (LIVE ANIMAL) — A sealed cardboard
box labeled LIVE ANIMAL. Motionless. Possibly
empty. Possibly occupied. Possibly neither. (Never
speaks.)

SETTING

A quiet front porch.
A cardboard box sits center stage.
It reads in bold lettering: LIVE ANIMAL.
There is no address.

*(Lights dim. A faint hum of insects. GIRL and BOY
stand on either side of the box.)*

GIRL
Is that you?

BOY
No way.

GIRL
I wonder what's in it.

BOY
Well—

it says
"LIVE ANIMAL."

(Silence — 7 seconds. City hum in the distance.)

GIRL
I don't hear anything.

(Pause — 3 seconds.)

BOY
Maybe it's dead.

GIRL
"LIVE ANIMAL".

(Silence — 10 seconds. The box remains perfectly still.)

BOY
It's bait.

*(Silence — 5 seconds. Then BOY produces duck calls.
At first brief, then extended — about 12 seconds.
He stops. Long pause — 8 seconds.)*

GIRL
(confused)
What makes you think it's a duck?

BOY
That was trap—
not a duck.
(Silence — 6 seconds.)

GIRL
It's addressed—

(She examines the label closely.)

—to no one.

BOY
Lacuna! Of course it was Lacuna!

GIRL
That little—

BOY
Right?

GIRL
Took your wallet.

BOY
Sent a decoy.

GIRL
And now we're being hunted.

BOY
By a dead duck.

*(GIRL begins mimicking duck calls toward the sky.
BOY gestures, giving clipped instructions.)*

BOY
(pointing at the box)
Aim it here!
(beat)
Louder!
(beat)
Jump!
(beat)
Okay stop!

(Long silence — 12 seconds. Insects buzz faintly.)

BOY
Maybe it's dead.

GIRL
"Live Animal."

(They both stare at the box in silence — 6 seconds.)

GIRL
(nodding no)
It's both.

(Silence — 5 seconds.)

BOY
Uncertainty.

(Pause — 3 seconds.)

GIRL
(nodding yes)
A myth.
Mist.

BOY
A coin lost in the gutter.

(She kneels beside the box, voice softening, intimate.
Her words now broken into breath and fragments.)

GIRL
It's me.
(small silence)
Between moments.
Here—
and not.

(pause — 4 seconds)

A stitch of presence.
Then the seam.

(pause — 5 seconds)

A sigh.

She wants—
essence.

(silence — 6 seconds)

No name.

No face.

Just a string
waiting to hum.

(pause — 5 seconds)

Drift.
Keep drifting.

BOY
Two particles, walking together—
One asks the other, "Where are you going?"
The other shrugs, "Not sure."
(beat — he chuckles, surprised)
"I'll let you know."

(They look at the box for a beat — 15 seconds.
The silence feels tender but uneasy.
A faint rustle comes from inside — ambiguous, almost
imagined.)

(Blackout.)

The Sarah Desert

An Absurdist Monologue

CHARACTERS

SPEAKER – A meticulously dressed traveler whose devotion to logic
has metastasized into ritualized certainty.

SETTING

A narrow room. A single suitcase rests on a bench.
A full winter ensemble — scarf, peacoat, boots,
mi**ttens — worn indoors.**
The speaker addresses no one and everyone.

SPEAKER
I am wearing a waffle long sleeve
beneath a chunky rope-knit sweater
beneath a sheepland peacoat.

(beat)
For a reason.

(beat)
A very—
good…
reason.

(pause)
One that too few people are capable of reasoning.

Why?
Well…
(pause)
Because people—
are—

reasonably unreasonable,
and lack the reasoning required
for a reason.

(*beat*)
That's a fact.
And that—
is the problem with our society today.

People have become—
dumb—
and numb.

(*pause*)
Maybe it's in the air.
Maybe it's in the water.
Or worse—
maybe it's in their genes .

Stupidity—
woven in—
like twill.

(*long pause*)
These trousers?
Mohair.
A fur extracted from the genius Mohairis Genetica.
Exceptional warmth.

(*beat*)
By the way—
if you were inquisitive—
(which you are not)—

you'd ask:
What gives?

Well.
Let me tell you a little story.
(pause)
I'm about to visit a friend
in a land
called
The Sarah Desert.

(beat)
Somewhere in Africa, I believe.

(beat)
We're going to a concert.
A band called Rush.

(beat)
I checked the weather.
One hundred seventeen times.

(pause)
Why 117?
Because I do not overpack.
I do not underpack.
I pack
precisely
what can fit
in a backpack.
Avoid overweight charges.
Maintain efficiency.
Be civilized.

(pause)
I will leave at 8 ante meridian
specific pacific time—
not a minute more
or less—
or I risk being late
by a minute or two.

That is not how I operate.

(beat)
I called the cab company two months ago
and reserved eight cars—
just in case
any one of them
is late
or
not on time.

(pause)
The price is no matter.
No matter the price.
Money is no object
when it comes to prices that matter.

(beat)
Punctuality!

First rule of show business.
Write it down.
This is wisdom you people could benefit from.
(beat)

You are NOT inquisitive, remember?

(beat)
If it had teeth,
it would bite you.

(pause, shifting tone)
"The weather in sunny Sarah today will be hot and
humid — as it was for the last week."

(beat)
Bingo.

(beat)
So what do I do?

(pause, relishing)
I put on the heaviest winter gear
I can dig out of my closet.

(pause)
If you were inquisitive—
(which you are not)—
you'd ask again:
What gives?

(beat)
Let's talk math.

Suppose you're at the roulette table.
Black hits 117 times in a row.

Do you bet on black again?

(pause, leans forward)
C'mon…

Get a brain, people.
Get a life.

I have a flight to catch.
Eight cabs.
All on time.

And when I step into The Sarah Desert—
bundled, prepared, civilized—
I will not sweat.
Not once.
Because chance…
cannot touch me.

(beat, soft smile)
Stay warm.

(Blackout.)

The Catch—22
A Short Absurdist Raffle Monologue

CHARACTERS

SPOKESPERSON – Slick, smiling, oily. Half confidence man, half evangelical motivational speaker. Wears a gaudy "WINNER" ribbon.
CROOK – Silent assistant. Moves ropes, waves people forward, smiles too wide.

SETTING

A stage decorated with balloons, a raffle drum, and a velvet rope. A table with no prize. The air smells faintly of chicken salad.

(Lights up. The SPOKESPERSON steps forward, arms wide. CROOK stands near the rope, watchful, smiling.)

SPOKESPERSON
Welcome, everyone!
I want to thank you all
for helping Resol
hit our financial goal—
one million bucks!

(pauses for imagined applause; CROOK claps once, too loudly, then stops)

I speak for all of us at Resol:
Crook,
Marauder,
and myself included—
when I say
we are—
quite literally, might I add—

74

very fortunate.

Your raffle money
will—metaphorically speaking—
raise our children,
pay for heat,
buy the wifey pearls,
and philosophically speaking—
drive us out of here
in a brand-new luxury automobile.

(claps once, sharp; CROOK echoes it, softer)

All this—
thanks to you.

Now then—
let's move on—
to! the! raffle!!

(drum roll… then silence. SPOKESPERSON leans into mic, grave.)

Pragamathematically speaking—
I've got
unfortunate news.

(shuffles cards)

It seems…
the prize—
the new luxury car we promised—
(turns over card, solemn)

…has been stolen.

That's right folks.
Gone.

(pats chest reassuringly)

Don't let your engines overheat.
Resol is gobsmacked
to make this right.

(snaps fingers; CROOK drags velvet rope into place,
creating a short "refund line")

If anyone here today
requested an interview
yesterday,
or the day before today,
or—today—
because you knew
this was going to happen…

(squints at the audience, mock-serious)

By the way,
nobody could metaphysically fathom
that anything like this could happen,
right?
Well then—
knowing that you didn't,
is proof.
Proof!

(beat. smile fades slightly)

If no interview was requested—
a refund
shan't be given.

*(gestures grandly toward CROOK, who bows and pats
his pocket as if holding envelopes)*

Resol will be enchanted
to provide a refund.
Just form a line here.
Crook will take good care of you.
Promise.

(beat. CROOK waits. Silence. Nobody moves.)

No requests, heh?

(grins coldly)

I am…
flaggerblasted.
*(claps hands once, sharp; CROOK jumps, then freezes
back into smile)*
Well—
those are the brakes, folks.

(steps forward slowly, lowering voice)

Though some say
the brakes were never installed.
Others say

the ride is still going.
And me?

(philosophical smile)

I'm just here
to announce the winners.

*(lifts empty envelope. Long silence. CROOK leans in,
staring at the emptiness.)*

Which, metaphorically speaking,
includes everyone here.

(leans into mic; pause)

Especially—

(beat, colder)

the losers.

*(Blackout. CROOK keeps smiling in the dark. The smell
of chicken salad lingers.)*

(Blackout.)

The Infinity Theater
A short absurdist dialogue in three movements

CHARACTERS

HELIX – A seeker. Curious, earnest, and eventually unraveling.
MAN 1 – Polite but nonsensical.
MAN 2 – Mocking, sardonic.
WOMAN – Wistful, wandering, obsessed with the past.
VOICE (Optional: use HELIX or prerecorded) – Delivers Poetic Preludes.

SETTING

A surreal street corner. Fog drifts across the stage. A flickering lamppost leans overhead. A kiosk labeled "Infinity Theater – Box Office" buzzes faintly but remains unmanned. The air carries déjà vu

Poetic Prelude I

HELIX (*narrating*)
Longing
is a hand—
reaching
for a door,
that's always
just
closing.

Scene I

HELIX
Excuse me, sir—
which way to the Infinity Theater?

MAN 1
Any which-way paths
will do, sir.

HELIX
That's impossible.

MAN 1
Precisely.

HELIX
Thanks anyway.

(Exit HELIX.)

Poetic Prelude II

HELIX *(narrating)*
Neither words,
nor music—
suffice.
Information
created—
inside
invisible.

Scene II

HELIX
Excuse me, sir—
how do I get to the Infinity Theater?

MAN 2
Ha!
Is this a joke?

HELIX
Not a jo—

MAN 2
You must have knotted your brain in loops.

HELIX
And you, sir, are a—

MAN 2
Yeah, yeah, yeah.
Good luck chasing infinity—
looper!

(Exit HELIX.)

Poetic Prelude III

HELIX *(narrating)*
Memory drips
from the knuckles—
salted,
stung,
never held.

Scene III

HELIX *(approaching)*
Excuse me, ma'am—

WOMAN
Yes?

HELIX
So sorry to bother you—
I need to get to the—

WOMAN
Simmer down, young man,
just simmer down now…

HELIX
…Infinity—

WOMAN
Theater?

HELIX *(calmer)*
Yes.

(long silence)

WOMAN
…Got a smoke?

HELIX
I… don't smoke.

WOMAN
Young man—
I asked you for a cigarette,
not your reason for declining.

HELIX
Yes, and I—

WOMAN
Do you?

HELIX
…No.

WOMAN
Loops…

(long silence)

WOMAN
That's life, I suppose.
Cigarettes are no good.
Goodness knows,
I ought to quit.
For the good.
For good.

Nothing like a good smoke,
particularly with good Italian espresso—
no other does it for me quite the same.
Ristretto!
With no sugar—
a shot of sambuca stirred in,
and that cigarette—
wheeeeeew…

(silence.)

Loops…
The good ol' days…
That's life, I suppose.

(pause)

That's…

(pause)

The Infinity Theater.

(long silence)

Proceed half the way,
then a quarter,
an eighth…

HELIX
Yes—
subsequently?

WOMAN
A sixteenth,
thirty-second,
sixty-fourth
one-twenty-eighth,
one-two-hundred-fifty-sixth…

(She continues. Endlessly .)

HELIX
Excuse me, ma'am—
which way to the Infinity Theater?

(Blackout.)

The Man With No Birthday
A Short Absurdist Play

CHARACTERS

JOEY — An earnest organizer. Well-meaning, verbal, increasingly unsettled. Speaks as if clarity might stabilize reality.
HARRY — Calm, polite, unsettlingly serene. A man without origin, documentation, or proof of arrival.
THE GUESTS — A silent gathering. Friends, acquaintances, or placeholders. Their presence is implied more than confirmed.
THE EMPTY CHAIR — An unoccupied folding chair. Bears a faint stain. May be evidence. (Does not speak.)

SETTING

A dim community center banquet hall. Folding chairs, paper cups, and a sagging banner: "Happy Birthday." The room is too quiet.

(Long silence. JOEY steps forward, clutching a paper cup. He clears his throat.)

JOEY
Alright, everyone. Thanks for coming.

I just found out Harry is having a birthday next month,
so I gathered us here today
to give you some information—about Harry's party.

Harry is a dear friend of the family.
That just means—he's not a co-worker.

Co-workers, by definition,
aren't quite "dear."
Though they do have birthdays.

Slightly more "dear" than an associate, I'd say.

Now "neighbor"—
that's a doozy of a word.
Whole other ball of hair.

Neighbors usually—though not always—live next
door.
But sometimes it's two doors over.
Still counts.

Anyway—
"dear" applies.
Don't be afraid to use it.

But Harry—
he isn't my neighbor.
Nor my co-worker.

Harry is just—
a dear friend.

And I'm thrilled to tell you:
Harry is having a birthday.

(pause. Joey looks around the room. Drops voice.)

There's just…
one little problem.

Harry—
doesn't exist.

(beat)

No. Harry.
Not dead.
Just never existed.
Not in the typical sense.

Matter of fact,
I'll bet a few of you don't exist either.
You know who you are.
Let's not kid ourselves.

Now—
rather than explain—
I figured we'd hear it from the horse's mouth.

No offense, Harry.

Ladies and gentlemen—
the man of the hour.
Get on up here, Harry!

———

HARRY
(enters calmly, quiet smile)
Hi everyone.
It's true.
Everything Joey said—

all true.

(pause)

I don't remember my birthday.
Nobody alive does.

The doctor,
the nurse,
my mom,
my dad—
all gone.
And the hospital?
Burned to the ground.
No records.
No birth certificate.
No evidence.

(beat)

Imagine:
you're nestled in a blanket,
fire crackling,
reading Keats,
sipping brandy—
and wham!
Someone sticks a plunger on your skull
and yanks you into reality—

(silence, heavy)

—but not into existence.
I'm not even here.

So—
what exactly are we celebrating?

A memory
that can't remember.

JOEY
(quietly)
Well, there you have it.
Harry is a ghost.

(raises cup)

A toast—to Harry.
He was a good man,
and will be remembered.

Right, Harry?

HARRY
A dear friend.

JOEY
Not just a neighbor.
Not even real.
(beat)
But still—
he had better attendance
than most of you.

(beat. Joey scans the room, leans in.)
And if he never existed…

(points suddenly; light shifts onto an empty chair)

Tell me why there's an extra chair
with blood
on the cushion.

(Blackout.)

A Note on These Plays

These plays are not puzzles to be solved.
They are situations to be entered.

They do not ask what a character means, but
what a system does when followed faithfully.
Most of the figures you'll meet are not people
in the psychological sense—they are habits,
procedures, rationalizations, rituals, or
assurances speaking out loud.

Logic is taken at its word.
Courtesy is honored past usefulness.
Authority is obeyed until it contradicts itself.

Absurdity here is not exaggeration. It is
accumulation.

Many scenes repeat, stall, loop, or quietly
refuse to move forward. This is intentional.
Progress is not guaranteed. Resolution is not
promised. Meaning, when it appears, is usually
incidental.

Silence matters. Timing matters. What is not
said often carries more weight than what is.

These plays may be staged simply or
elaborately, but they do not require
explanation, interpretation, or apology. If
something feels unresolved, let it remain so. If
something feels obvious, resist clarifying it.

The work trusts the audience.
It also trusts the performer.

Everything else is optional.

Author's Note

These plays were written to be read aloud—
whether to an audience, a room, or oneself.

They are built from repetition, interruption,
misalignment, and pause. Meaning is not
always carried by plot or resolution, but by
rhythm, escalation, and collapse. Silence is not
absence here; it is an active force. A pause may
be longer than feels comfortable. That
discomfort is part of the work.

Characters in these plays are not always people
in a psychological sense. They may function as
roles, pressures, habits, or systems. Names can
be exchanged. Genders can be reassigned.
Doubling is encouraged. What matters is not
realism, but clarity of tension.

Time is elastic. Logic is negotiable.
Contradictions are not mistakes—they are
engines.

These plays do not ask to be solved. They ask
to be staged, spoken, endured, and allowed to
loop. If something feels unresolved, it probably
is. If something feels familiar, it may not belong
to you alone.

Read them straight. Read them funny. Read
them deadpan. Read them wrong.
Just don't rush the silence.

Performance Notes

These plays are designed for performance, but not decoration.

1. Tone

Most scenes work best underplayed. The comedy does not come from jokes, but from commitment—to faulty logic, rigid habits, bureaucratic language, or emotional certainty. The flatter the delivery, the sharper the fracture.

If something feels "too absurd," it is usually being pushed. Pull back.

2. Pace & Silence

Silence is structural.

Pauses are not placeholders for emotion—they are the emotion. A pause may be uncomfortable. Let it be. Do not fill silence with gesture, explanation, or apology.

If a pause feels too long, it is probably correct.

3. Characters

Characters are not psychological case studies.
They function as pressures, positions, or
systems:

a rule enforcing itself
a habit defending itself
a logic arguing with reality

Backstory is optional. Consistency of behavior
is not.

Names may be reassigned. Gender is flexible
unless otherwise specified. Doubling roles is
encouraged.

4. Escalation

Most scenes escalate by repetition with
variation, not by raising volume or intensity.

The performer's job is to repeat sincerely—
even as the logic collapses. The audience will
track the shift; the character should not.

5. Authority

Many characters speak with institutional
confidence—clerks, professionals, hosts,
experts. This authority should feel casual, not

villainous. The more reasonable the tone, the more unsettling the outcome.

6. Props & Set

Minimalism is preferred.

A single object should carry weight (a form, a box, a cake, a thermostat). Avoid realism that explains too much. If an object must be imaginary, commit fully.

7. Endings & Blackouts

Endings do not resolve. They stop.

A blackout is not punctuation—it is termination.
No button. No wink. No release.

If the final line lands hard, let the darkness arrive immediately. If the final line drifts, allow the silence to do the work.

8. Failure

If a scene feels like it is failing—flat, stalled, circular—it may be working correctly.

Stay with it.